THE PLANETARY SOCIETY

DWARF PLANETS

SMALL ROUND WORLDS

Bruce Betts, PhD

Lerner Publications ◆ Minneapolis

THE PLANETS AND MOONS IN OUR SOLAR SYSTEM ARE OUT OF THIS WORLD. Some are hotter than an oven, and some are much colder than a freezer. Some are small and rocky, while others are huge and mostly made of gas. As you explore these worlds, you'll discover giant canyons, active volcanoes, strange kinds of ice, storms bigger than Earth, and much more.

The Planetary Society® empowers people around the world to advance space science and exploration. On behalf of The Planetary Society®, including our tens of thousands of members, here's wishing you the joy of discovery.

Onward,

Bill Nye

Bill Nye
CEO, The Planetary Society®

TABLE OF CONTENTS

CHAPTER 1

WHAT IS A DWARF PLANET?

Our solar system is everything that goes around the Sun. This includes the eight planets and five dwarf planets. Ceres, Pluto, Eris, Makemake, and Haumea are the dwarf planets.

Ceres is in the asteroid belt between Mars and Jupiter. The other four dwarf planets spend most of their time past Neptune. Neptune is the farthest planet from the Sun.

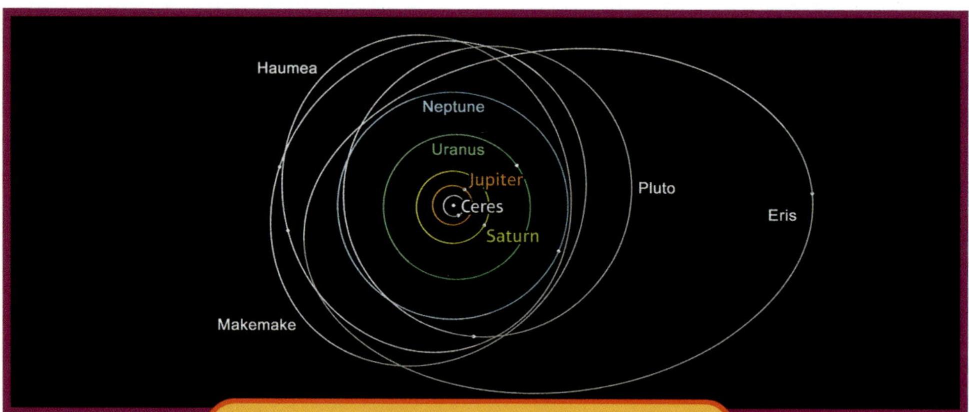

The paths of the dwarf planets (*white*) and the paths of outer planets (*colors*)

Planets and dwarf planets are similar. They all go around the Sun. They can also have moons. Moons are rocky or icy objects that go around other objects such as planets.

DWARF PLANETS FAST FACTS

Ceres
- Smallest dwarf planet
- Found in the asteroid belt between Mars and Jupiter

Pluto
- Largest dwarf planet
- Spends most of its time beyond Neptune

Eris
- Highest mass of all the dwarf planets
- Dwarf planet that goes the farthest from the Sun

Makemake
- Second smallest dwarf planet
- Reddish color

Haumea
- Shaped like an American football or a rugby ball
- Dwarf planet with shortest day of about four hours

Planets vs. Dwarf Planets

Planets and dwarf planets both are big and round like a ball. They are round because they have strong gravity that pulls them into a ball shape. Gravity is what holds you down on Earth. But planets and dwarf planets have one big difference.

Real photos of Pluto and Ceres, and drawings of Eris, Haumea, and Makemake

A diagram of the asteroid belt

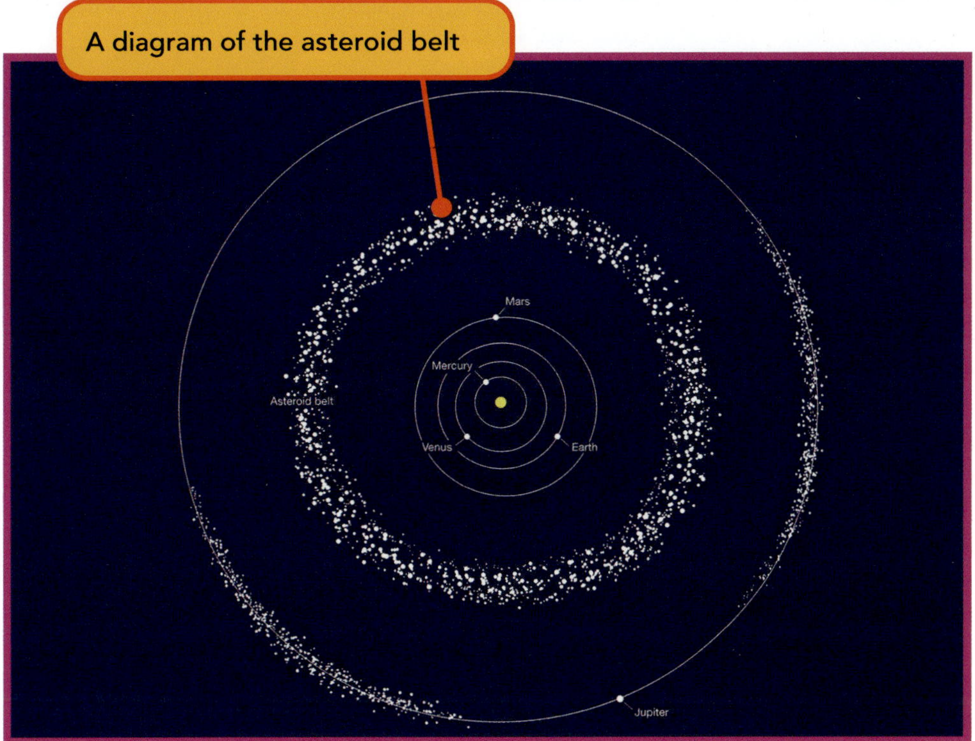

In 2006, scientists decided on a new rule for a space object to be called a planet. The rule is that nothing of similar size to the planet can be near its orbit. An orbit is the path a planet, moon, or other object follows as it goes around another object.

This new rule led to the invention of the term *dwarf planet*. Dwarf planets *do* have objects of similar size near or in their orbits. For example, Ceres and millions of other objects are in the asteroid belt. Since some of the objects are similar in size to Ceres, Ceres is not a planet.

CHAPTER 2

CERES

Scientist Giuseppe Piazzi discovered Ceres in 1801. It was the first object spotted between Mars and Jupiter. It was called a planet for many years.

This telescope discovered Ceres.

More rocky bodies were found in that area of space, which was later named the asteroid belt. Ceres and those objects in the belt were then called asteroids. But Ceres has been called a dwarf planet since the term was first created in 2006.

Ceres is the smallest dwarf planet. But it is the largest object in the asteroid belt. It is about 584 miles (939 km) wide. Ceres is the only object in the asteroid belt that is round. Ceres has no moons.

A color picture of Ceres from the Dawn spacecraft

Ceres the Goddess

Ceres is named after the Roman goddess of grains and harvests. The word *cereal* also comes from Ceres.

Ceres is almost three times farther from the Sun than Earth is. It is very cold compared to Earth. It has a thin atmosphere that may have some water vapor.

Ceres takes almost five Earth years to go around the Sun. That is a Ceres year. It spins around in about nine hours. That is the length of a Ceres day.

Ceres (*bottom left*) is much smaller than Earth's Moon (*top left*) and Earth.

This drawing shows the Dawn spacecraft above Ceres.

Impact craters on Ceres

Surface of Ceres

The Dawn spacecraft began orbiting and taking pictures of Ceres in 2015. Dawn discovered that Ceres looks similar to Earth's Moon. Ceres has many impact craters all over its surface. They were formed by asteroids slamming into Ceres at high speeds.

Bright areas in Occator Crater on Ceres

Ceres is mostly gray with some bright white spots. Scientists think the spots are caused by salts. They might form from salty liquid water coming out from below the surface. When the water disappears, salty materials from the water stay.

Ceres also has mountains. Its largest mountain is called Ahuna Mons. It is about 16,000 feet (5,000 m) high. Scientists think Ahuna Mons formed from water ice, salt, and mud coming out of the surface at very cold temperatures.

This image of Ahuna Mons was made from photos taken by Dawn.

CHAPTER 3

PLUTO

Scientist Clyde Tombaugh discovered Pluto in 1930. Over time, it was discovered that Pluto was much smaller than any of the other planets and in a much different orbit.

Pluto was called a planet until 2006. Scientists then saw that Pluto had many other objects of similar size near its orbit. So they decided it would be called a dwarf planet instead.

This color image of Pluto's surface shows mountains and impact craters.

Pluto is the largest dwarf planet in our solar system. It spends most of its time beyond Neptune. The New Horizons spacecraft flew by Pluto in 2015. It gave us our only close-up view of Pluto and its moons.

Pluto is about forty times farther from the Sun than Earth is. It took New Horizons almost ten years to get to Pluto.

Pluto in true color

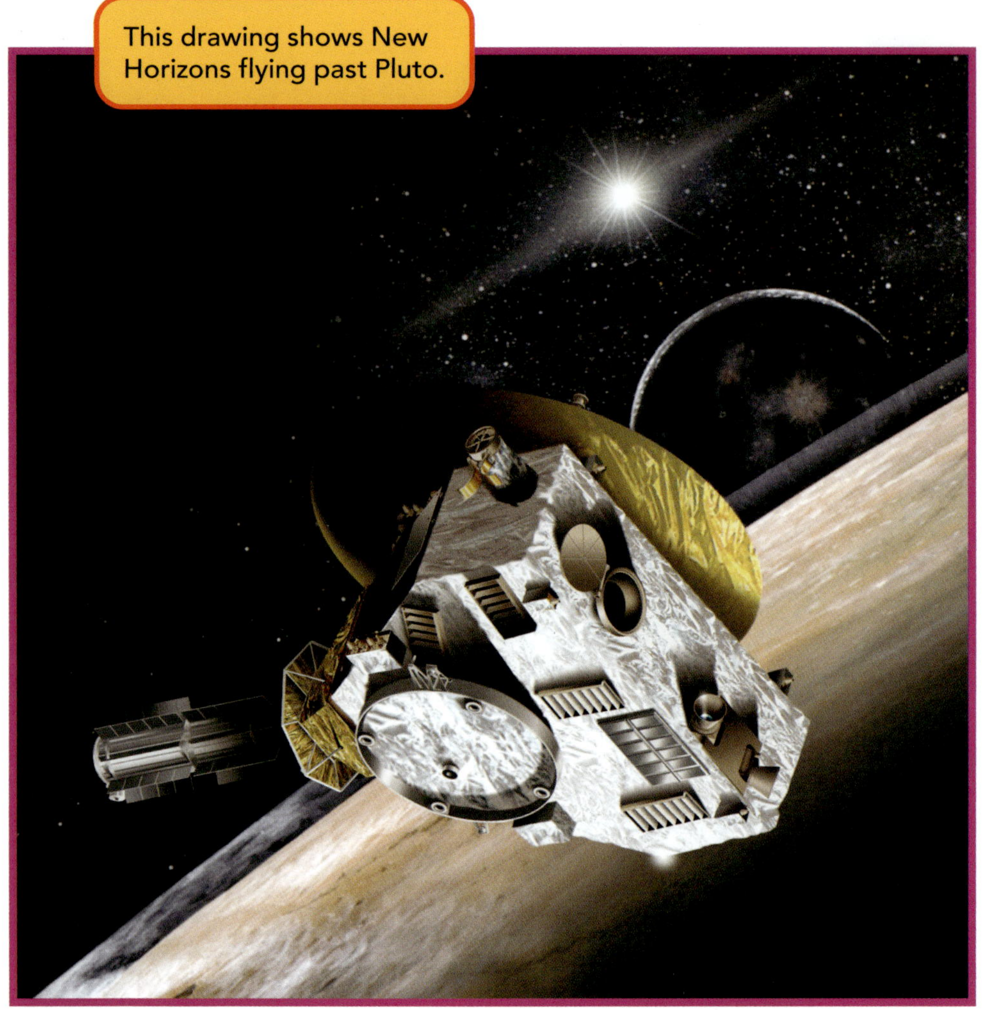

This drawing shows New Horizons flying past Pluto.

Temperature, Ice, and More

Pluto is far from the Sun and is very cold. It takes 248 Earth years for Pluto to go around the Sun. A Pluto day is a little longer than six Earth days.

Naming Pluto

Pluto was named after the Roman god of the underworld. The name was suggested by an eleven-year-old girl. All of Pluto's moons are named after things in Roman and Greek mythology.

Pluto is about two-thirds as wide as Earth's Moon. The dwarf planet would stretch about halfway across the United States.

Pluto has a very thin atmosphere. Its surface is mostly a reddish color.

The size of Pluto (*bottom left*) compared to Earth and Earth's Moon (*top left*)

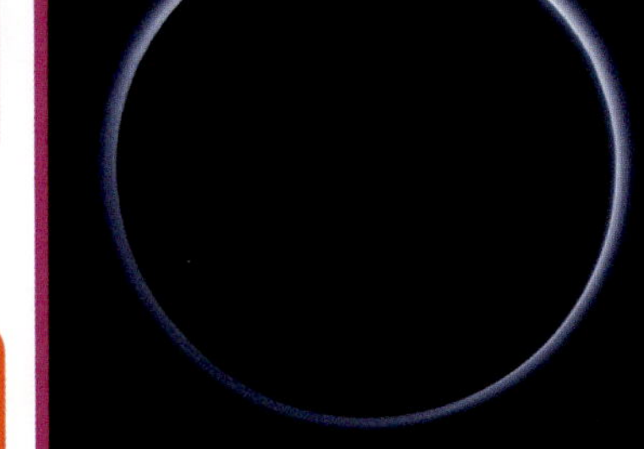

Pluto's thin atmosphere looks blue when lit by the Sun.

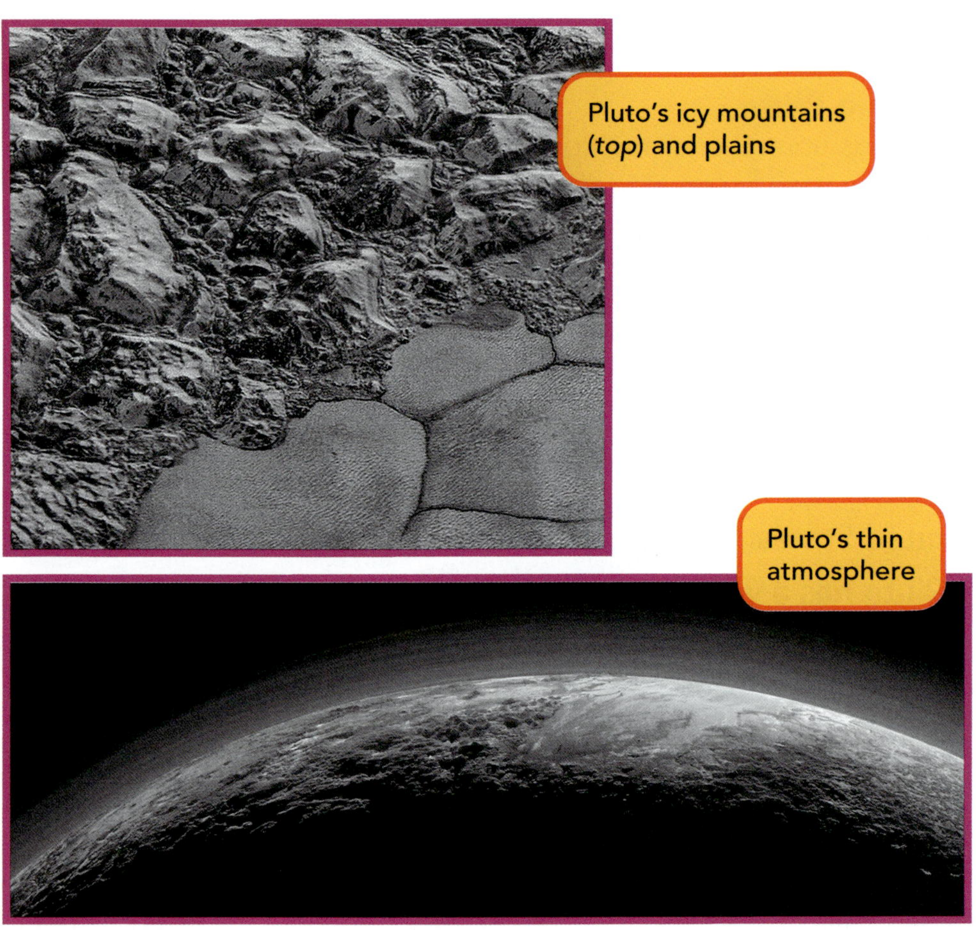

Pluto is covered in ices. It is so cold that water ice forms mountains. Other things also freeze there because it is so cold.

Methane is a gas on Earth. But it forms ice caps on Pluto on some of the water ice mountains. Other ices form flat plains. Some of that ice moves very slowly over time.

CHARON

Pluto has at least five moons. Charon is its largest moon. The other moons are very small. Charon is half as wide as Pluto. Charon has some very large canyons. Canyons are big, long holes in the ground.

Pluto spins at the same speed as Charon goes around it. Because of this, only one side of Pluto ever sees the moon. If you were to stand on Pluto, Charon would stay in the same spot in the sky all the time.

Pluto's moon Charon in color

CHAPTER 4

ERIS, MAKEMAKE, AND HAUMEA

The dwarf planets Eris, Makemake, and Haumea are all very far away. They look like dots even in pictures taken by large telescopes. Spacecraft have never visited any of them.

All eight of the planets and Ceres orbit in one flat disk. These three dwarf planets and Pluto do not.

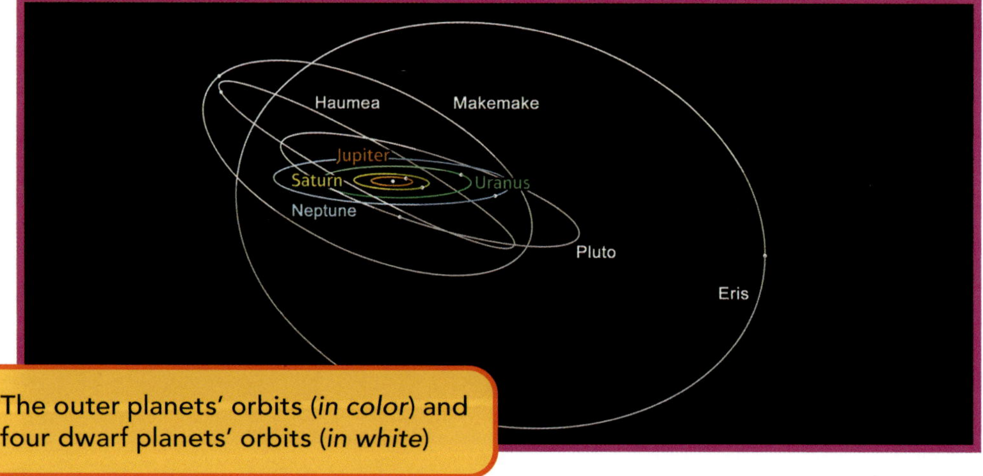

The outer planets' orbits (*in color*) and four dwarf planets' orbits (*in white*)

Eris

Eris was discovered in 2005. It is almost the same size as Pluto. Other nearly Pluto-sized objects were also found beyond Neptune around that time. These facts led to the decision that Pluto, Eris, and Ceres should be called dwarf planets instead of planets.

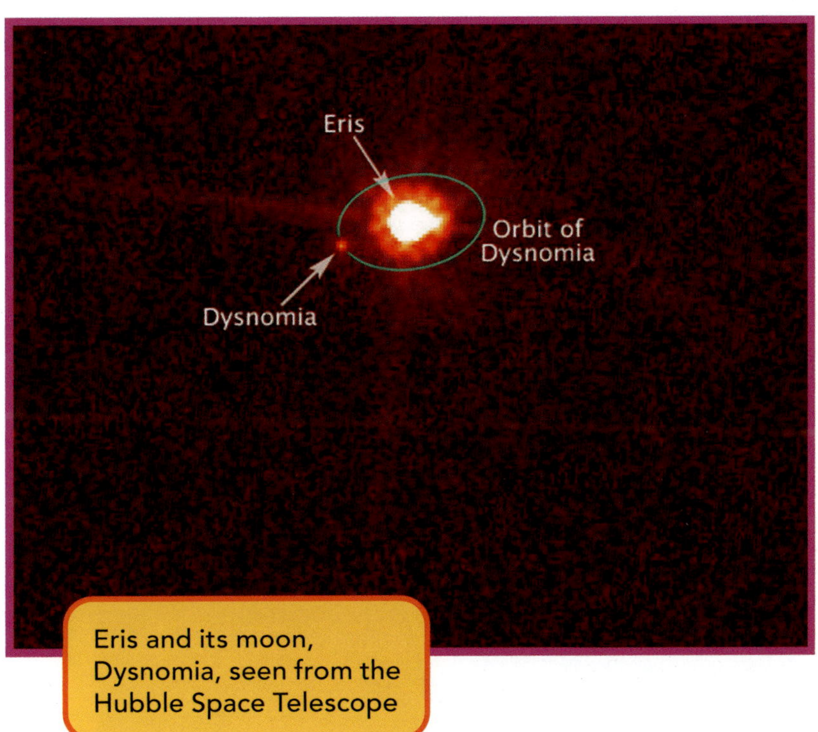

Eris and its moon, Dysnomia, seen from the Hubble Space Telescope

Planet or Dwarf Planet?
Eris was named after the Greek goddess of arguments. Eris caused a lot of arguments over the meaning of the word *planet* and led to the invention of the term *dwarf planet*.

Even though Eris and Pluto are similar in size, Eris is the dwarf planet with the most mass. That means it's the heaviest.

It takes Eris about 557 Earth years to orbit the Sun! It goes almost one hundred times farther from the Sun than Earth does. Its orbit is very tilted compared to the planets' orbits.

A drawing of Eris and its moon, Dysnomia (*top*)

This drawing shows the bright surface of Eris (*left*) and the dark surface of Dysnomia.

Eris spins around about once every sixteen days. Eris has one moon called Dysnomia. Dysnomia also orbits Eris in about sixteen days. Like Pluto and Charon, the moon can only be seen from one side of the dwarf planet.

Makemake

Makemake was also first seen in 2005. It is almost two-thirds as wide as Pluto or Eris. It is a similar reddish-brown color to Pluto.

Makemake is usually more than forty-five times farther from the Sun than Earth is. Its year is 305 Earth years long. Its day is about twenty-three hours.

A drawing of Makemake and its moon (*right*)

A Hubble Space Telescope image of Makemake and its moon, MK 2 (*top*)

One moon has been discovered around Makemake. It is much smaller and darker than Makemake. Makemake is named after the Rapa Nui creation god. Its moon is nicknamed MK 2.

Haumea

Haumea is a weird object. It is one of the fastest spinning objects in the solar system. Its day is only four hours long.

Haumea's fast spin made it stretch out. It is shaped like an American football or a rugby ball. It is about as long as Pluto, but only about half as wide.

Haumea has a ring of rocks, dust, and maybe ice around it.

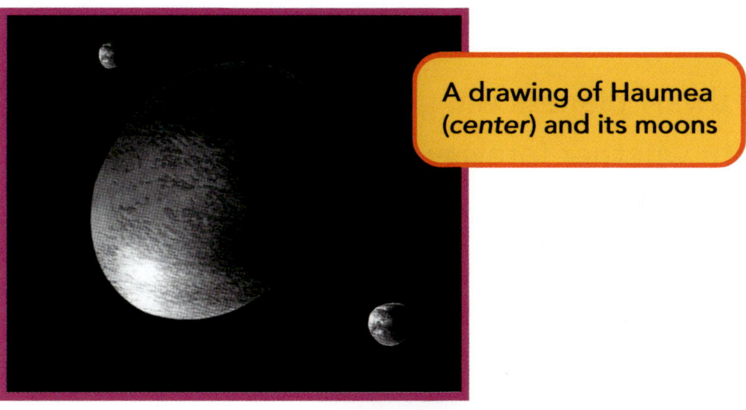

A drawing of Haumea (*center*) and its moons

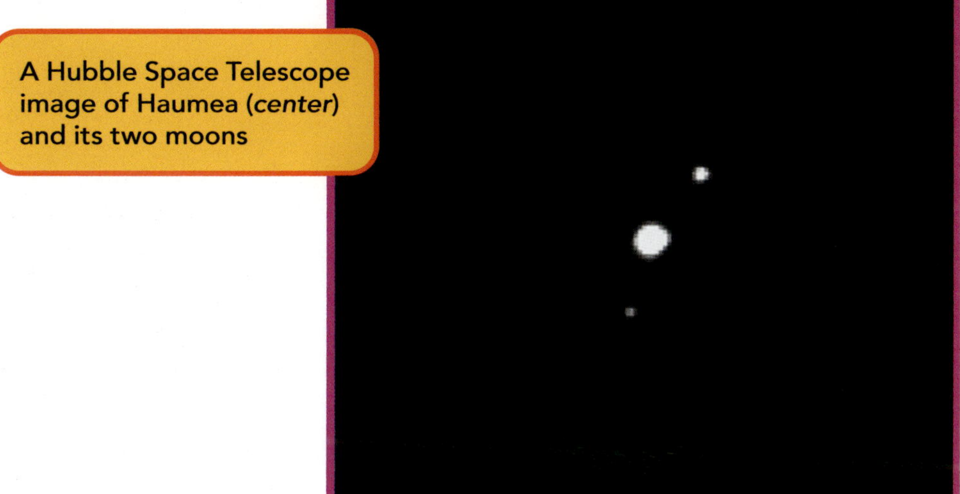

A Hubble Space Telescope image of Haumea (*center*) and its two moons

Haumea takes 285 Earth years to orbit the Sun. It is more than about forty times farther from the Sun than Earth is.

Haumea has two known moons. Namaka is the inner moon. Hi'iaka is the outer moon. This dwarf planet and its moons are named after a Hawaiian goddess and her daughters.

The Future

The number of dwarf planets will get bigger in the future. It is hard to learn whether faraway objects have been made round by gravity as dwarf planets need to be. Scientists are talking about which space objects should be called dwarf planets. New powerful telescopes will also discover new objects, some of which will be dwarf planets.

A drawing of the James Webb Space Telescope that was launched in late 2021 and is helping to study dwarf planets

The rocket launching New Horizons in 2006 on its way to Pluto

Glossary

atmosphere: the gases surrounding a planet, moon, or other object in space

day: the time it takes a planet or moon to spin around and go from noon to noon. One Earth day is about twenty-four hours.

dwarf planet: a round, ball-shaped object that only goes around the Sun. A dwarf planet has objects close to the same size near its orbit.

impact crater: a bowl-shaped hole caused by a space rock hitting the ground at a high speed

mass: the total amount of matter that makes up an object

orbit: the path a planet, moon, or other object follows as it goes around another object

planet: a big, round, ball-shaped object that only goes around the Sun. Our solar system has eight planets. A planet does not have anything close to the same size near its orbit.

year: the time it takes a space object to go all the way around the Sun. One Earth year is about 365 days.

Learn More

Betts, Bruce, PhD. *Asteroids and Comets: Orbiting Space Rocks*. Minneapolis: Lerner Publications, 2025.

NASA Space Place: All about Pluto
https://spaceplace.nasa.gov/all-about-pluto/en/

National Geographic Kids: Dwarf Planets
https://kids.nationalgeographic.com/space/article/dwarf-planets

Planets for Kids: Dwarf Planets
https://www.planetsforkids.org/dwarf-planet.html

Ringstad, Arnold. *Dwarf Planets*. Mankato, MN: Child's World, 2020.

Schuh, Mari C. *Pluto and Other Dwarf Planets: Small Objects around the Sun*. Minneapolis: Jump!, 2023.

Index

Photo Acknowledgments

Image credits: F. Scott Schafer/The Planetary Society, p. 2; NASA/JPL-Caltech/Bruce Betts, pp. 4, 20; NASA, p. 6; ESA/Hubble, M. Kornmesser, p. 7; NASA/JPL-Caltech/Palermo Observatory, p. 8; NASA/JPL-Caltech/UCLA/MPS/DLR/IDA, pp. 9, 11 (bottom), 12–13; NASA/JPL-Caltech/UCLA/MPS/DLR/IDA/Gregory H. Revera/Wikimedia Commons (PD), p. 10; NASA/JPL-Caltech, pp. 11 (top), 22; NASA/JHUAPL/SwRI, pp. 14–15, 17 (right), 18–19; NASA/Dan Durda/SwRI, p. 16; NASA/JHUAPL/SWRI/Gregory H. Revera/Wikimedia Commons (PD), p. 17 (left); NASA/ESA/M. Brown (Caltech), p. 21; ESO/L. Calçada and Nick Risinger/Wikimedia Commons (PD), p. 23; NASA/ESA/A. Parker (SwRI), p. 24; NASA/ESA/A. Parker and M. Buie (SwRI), p. 25; IAA-CSIC/UHU, p. 26; NASA/A. Feild (Space Telescope Science Institute)/Wikimedia Commons (PD), p. 27 (top); NASA/ESA/STScI/D. Ragozzine/Wikimedia Commons (PD), p. 27 (bottom); NASA/ESA/Hubble/Wikimedia Commons (PD), p. 28; NASA/Kim Shiflett/Wikimedia Commons (PD), p. 29.
Cover: NASA/JHUAPL/SwRI.

FOR MY SONS, KEVIN AND DANIEL, AND FOR ALL THE MEMBERS OF THE PLANETARY SOCIETY®

Copyright © 2025 by The Planetary Society®

All rights reserved. International copyright secured. No part of this book may be reproduced, stored in a retrieval system, or transmitted in any form or by any means—electronic, mechanical, photocopying, recording, or otherwise—without the prior written permission of Lerner Publishing Group, Inc., except for the inclusion of brief quotations in an acknowledged review.

Lerner Publications Company
An imprint of Lerner Publishing Group, Inc.
241 First Avenue North
Minneapolis, MN 55401 USA

For reading levels and more information, look up this title at www.lernerbooks.com.

Main body text set in Aptifer Sans LT Pro. Typeface provided by Linotype AG.

Editor: Angel Kidd **Designer:** Mary Ross **Photo Editor:** Angel Kidd
Lerner team: Sue Marquis

Library of Congress Cataloging-in-Publication Data

Names: Betts, Bruce, PhD, author.
Title: Dwarf planets : small round worlds / Bruce Betts, PhD.
Description: Minneapolis, MN : Lerner Publications, [2025] | Series: Exploring our solar system with the Planetary Society | Includes bibliographical references and index. | Audience: Ages 7–10 | Audience: Grades 2–3 | Summary: "There are five dwarf planets in our solar system. From Ceres to Eris, readers will learn about where the dwarf planets are found, the spacecraft that study them, and what makes them different from planets"— Provided by publisher.
Identifiers: LCCN 2024013843 (print) | LCCN 2024013844 (ebook) | ISBN 9798765648292 (library binding) | ISBN 9798765661741 (paperback) | ISBN 9798765654637 (epub)
Subjects: LCSH: Dwarf planets—Juvenile literature.
Classification: LCC QB698 .B48 2025 (print) | LCC QB698 (ebook) | DDC 523.44—dc23/eng/20240617

LC record available at https://lccn.loc.gov/2024013843
LC ebook record available at https://lccn.loc.gov/2024013844

Manufactured in the United States of America
1-1011034-53387-6/26/2024